GALATIANS

BRINGING THE BIBLE TO LIFE

Genesis, by John H. Walton, Janet Nygren, and Karen H. Jobes
(12 sessions)

Esther, by Karen H. Jobes and Janet Nygren
(8 sessions)

Psalms, by Gerald Wilson, Janet Nygren, and Karen H. Jobes
(10 sessions) — summer 2010

Daniel, by Tremper Longman III, Janet Nygren, and Karen H. Jobes
(10 sessions)

Mark, by David E. Garland, Karen-Lee Thorp, and Karen H. Jobes
(12 sessions)

John, by Gary M. Burge, Karen Lee-Thorp, and Karen H. Jobes
(12 sessions)

Acts, by Ajith Fernando, Karen Lee-Thorp, and Karen H. Jobes
(12 sessions) — summer 2010

Romans, by Douglas J. Moo, Karen Lee-Thorp, and Karen H. Jobes
(12 sessions)

Galatians, by Scot McKnight, Karen Lee-Thorp, and Karen H. Jobes
(6 sessions)

Ephesians, by Klyne Snodgrass, Karen Lee-Thorp, and Karen H. Jobes
(6 sessions)

Hebrews, by George H. Guthrie, Janet Nygren, and Karen H. Jobes
(8 sessions)

Revelation, by Craig S. Keener, Janet Nygren, and Karen H. Jobes
(10 sessions) — summer 2010

**BRINGING
THE
BIBLE
TO LIFE**

GALATIANS

Living in Freedom and Love

Scot McKnight
Karen Lee-Thorp

Karen H. Jobes, Series Editor

ZONDERVAN.com/
AUTHORTRACKER
follow your favorite authors

ZONDERVAN

Bringing the Bible to Life: Galatians
Copyright © 2010 by Scot McKnight, Karen Lee-Thorp, and Karen H. Jobes

Requests for information should be addressed to:

Zondervan, *Grand Rapids, Michigan 49530*

ISBN 978-0-310-32045-6

Cover design: Tammy Johnson
Cover and interior photography: iStockphoto
Interior design: Michelle Espinoza

Printed in the United States of America

09 10 11 12 13 14 15 • 26 25 24 23 22 21 20 19 18 17 16 15 14 13 12 11 10 9 8 7 6 5 4 3 2 1

CONTENTS

SERIES PREFACE

Have you ever been in a small-group Bible study where the leader read a passage from the Bible and then invited the members of the group to share what the passage meant to them? God wants to speak to each person individually through the Bible, but such an approach to a group study can often be a frustrating and shallow experience for both leader and participants. And while the same passage can speak in various ways into people's lives, the meat of the Word is found in what the biblical writer intended to say about God and our relationship to him. The Bringing the Bible to Life series is for those who are ready to move from a surface reading of the Bible into a deeper understanding of God's Word.

But the Bible, though perhaps familiar, was written in ancient languages and in times quite different from our own, so most readers need a bit more help getting to a deeper understanding of its message. A study that begins and ends with what a passage "means to me" leaves the meaning of the passage unanchored and adrift in the thoughts—and perhaps the misunderstanding—of the reader. But who has time to delve into the history, language, cultures, and theology of the Bible? That's the work of biblical scholars who spend their lives researching, teaching, and writing about the ancient Scriptures. The need is to get the fruit of all that research into the hands of those in small-group Bible studies.

Zondervan's NIV Application Commentary (NIVAC) series was written to bring the best of evangelical biblical scholarship to those who want to know *both* the historical meaning of the biblical text *and* its contemporary significance. This companion series, Bringing the Bible to Life, is intended to bring that material into small-group studies in an easy-to-use format. Pastors, Christian education teachers, and small-group leaders whether in church, campus, or home settings will find these guides to be an enriching resource.

Each guide in the series provides an introduction to the biblical book that concisely summarizes the background information needed to better understand the original historical context. Six to twelve sessions per guide, with each session generally consisting of ten to twelve discussion questions, allow a focused study that moves beyond superficial Bible reading. Relevant excerpts from the corresponding NIVAC commentary provide easy access into additional material for those interested in going even deeper. A closing section in each session assists the group in responding to God's Word together or individually. Guidance for leading each session is included, making the task of small-group leadership more manageable for busy lives.

If you want to move from the biblical text to contemporary life on solid ground, this series has been written for you.

Karen H. Jobes, PhD
Gerald F. Hawthorne Professor of
New Testament Greek and Exegesis
Wheaton College and Graduate School

OF SPECIAL NOTE

Your experience with and understanding of the book of Galatians can be deepened and enriched by referring to the volume on which it is based: *The NIV Application Commentary: Galatians* by Scot McKnight, published by Zondervan in 1995.

INTRODUCTION

CHRIST PLUS WHAT?

So you've put your faith in Christ and are saved by his gracious work on the cross. Now what? How do you live as a Christian? Swarms of churches, speakers, and books are available to tell you how. But there are two snares that even the most well-meaning church or teacher can fall into. You can fall into them all by yourself, alone in your room with your Bible.

The first snare is this: In order to make God really happy with the way you live as a Christian, you need Christ plus something else. It might be:

- Christ plus reading the right Bible translation
- Christ plus knowing the secrets of the end times
- Christ plus voting with the correct political party
- Christ plus practicing spiritual disciplines
- Christ plus working among the poor
- Christ plus protesting abortion
- Christ plus speaking in tongues (or *not* speaking in tongues)

These extras are often good, or at least neutral, in themselves. Our faith should influence our political choices. Spiritual disciplines like solitude and Bible study are invaluable. Abortion should be opposed. But sometimes these good things can become so much what *our* group is about—the thing that makes *our* group (or *my* spiritual life) better than *theirs*—that these good things eclipse Christ. A clue that we're sliding into this pitfall is if we're known more for these distinctives than for trusting Christ. And we're in big trouble if the "gospel" we communicate stops being "surrender to Christ" and becomes "join my group and do the things I do."

CAN THE HOLY SPIRIT BE TRUSTED?

The second, related, snare has to do with the Holy Spirit. We know God calls us to holiness, but receiving and acting on the Holy Spirit's guidance sometimes feels murky, uncertain. Beginners, in particular, can't be cut loose to listen to the Spirit, can they? It might be safer to have a list of good things to do (read your Bible, oppose abortion . . .) and a list of bad things not to do. At least that's clear. We may not live the robust, courageous life the Holy Spirit would call us to, but at least we'll do some good things and we won't mess up too badly.

THE GALATIANS

Here is roughly the scenario of what the young Christians in Galatia were facing in a time and place very different from ours. They were former pagans, and they knew the culture they'd grown up in had major problems. They knew they needed to live differently. Trusting that Christ's work and the guidance of the Holy Spirit would get them where they needed to go seemed scary (as it always does). And then messengers arrived from a faction of Jewish Christians in Jerusalem. These messengers — Bible scholars call them *Judaizers* — said what the Galatians needed was:

Christ plus the law of Moses — or more specifically,
Christ plus Moses' law as interpreted by an influential Jewish faction called the Pharisees.

It wasn't okay to be Christian Gentiles; they needed to be Christians plus Jews in the tradition of the Pharisaic rabbis. They needed to join the club and do what club members did. They needed to stop eating with their Gentile families and neighbors, and eat only with Jewish friends. They needed to abandon the culture and the people they'd grown up with and live in a subculture. Then God (and the Judaizers) would be happy with them.

PAUL

Enter the apostle Paul. It was he who had introduced the Galatians to the gospel in the first place (Acts 13 – 14). They were the first fruit of his missionary work. When he heard somebody was telling them they needed Christ plus Moses, he hit the ceiling. It didn't matter that he was himself a Jew with a deep knowledge of and respect for the law of Moses. Of course the law was good in itself. But he knew that Christ plus something else was spiritually lethal. So he wrote to his Galatian friends in a blistering letter telling them just how disastrous this altered "gospel" was. He wrote this letter in the late 40s AD, less than twenty years after Jesus' death and resurrection.

Paul himself had been trained among the Pharisees. Judaism was dizzyingly diverse in those days, and in Jerusalem the Pharisees were one of the most prominent groups. Some of them were even among the influential Jews in Jerusalem who had embraced Jesus as Messiah. But while Paul had learned much from the rabbis, he believed it was essential that their way of life not be imposed on non-Jewish believers. In Galatians, he explains why.

TWO MISUNDERSTANDINGS[1]

Two common misunderstandings of Galatians are worth correcting up front. First, as you probably know, Paul taught that we are saved by God's grace through faith in Christ. Period. As you may not know, the Judaizers agreed that they were saved by God's grace. Although Jews of the first century did not have unanimous views, in general they believed they were "saved" because they were God's elect people, not because they were capable of keeping the law perfectly. They kept the law as a response to God's gracious covenant with them, and when they sinned, they confessed and offered sacrifices to atone for sin.

Second, many people today believe the debate in Galatians is primarily about how you get saved, because Martin Luther focused on that important question five hundred years ago. But for Paul and the Judaizers, how you get saved isn't their main point of disagreement. It's what you do once you are saved. If Christ and the Holy Spirit were enough to bring you to salvation, are they enough for you to live the rest of your life in God's grace? Is the Holy Spirit enough to keep Christians away from lives of self-indulgence? Or is obedience to the Old Testament laws necessary too?

These are questions many of us struggle with day by day. Our hearts need to hear what Paul has to say.

NOTE

1. This section is based on *The NIV Application Commentary: Galatians* (hereafter referred to as *NIVAC: Galatians*) by Scot McKnight (Grand Rapids: Zondervan, 1995), 19–31.

THE REAL GOSPEL

Galatians 1:1–24

I n 1932, the German Christian movement took control of the German Evangelical Church and declared that Christians with Jewish ancestry could be considered Christians but not German Christians. They supported the Nazi call to cleanse Christianity of its focus on human sinfulness and other supposedly non-Aryan doctrines. The Nazis found the German Christians useful as they consolidated their power.

In 1933–1934, Christians who opposed Nazi ideas in the church drew increasing wrath from the state. Some leaders of the anti-Nazi Confessing Church movement were sent to concentration camps. While some Confessing Church members continued to risk their lives to help Jews, the majority of Christians in Germany either passively tolerated or actively supported a Nazi-tainted gospel. Some agreed with the tainted gospel; others feared persecution. After World War II, many Germans became cynical about Christianity because of the churches' weak response to Nazism.

While the "gospel" of Christ plus Aryan nationalism is more obviously evil to us than the "gospel" of Christ plus Jewish nationalism was to Christians in Paul's day, any tainted gospel contains the seeds of harm. Paul's Jewish kinsmen were understandably proud of their ethnic heritage, but when they tried to impose it on non-Jews, he responded in the strongest terms.

NOT OF HUMAN ORIGIN[1]

Read Galatians 1:1 – 17.

Paul writes to the Galatians to defend his gospel, and his first point is that his gospel "is not of human origin" (1:11). He "received it by revelation from Jesus Christ" (1:12). He is Christ's "apostle" (1:1) — that is, Christ's "personal agent, representative, or ambassador."[2] When God first gave him this gospel to proclaim, he didn't consult other humans, not even the apostles in Jerusalem (1:16 – 17). The Galatians need to know this, because the Judaizers have told them that Paul's gospel is incomplete or flawed and needs to be supplemented or overhauled.

1. What effect do you think Paul wanted his claim of divine authority (1:1) to have on the Galatians?

    How could the Galatians know whether Paul's gospel really did carry divine authority?

    How can we know today whether someone's teaching carries divine authority or is just a human invention?

If Paul's gospel really does carry the divine authority he claims, what are the implications for us today?

2. Paul doesn't completely spell out his gospel in this first chapter. However, what key elements of the gospel can we glean from 1:1 – 5 and 1:15 – 16?

The Judaizers' "different gospel" (1:6) alters the role Christ plays in a person's acceptance by God. It doesn't deny that Jesus is the Messiah, but it says that Gentiles need to both believe in Jesus as Messiah *and* live by the traditions of Moses as taught by the rabbis. It is Christ plus Moses, a cultural imperialism that says Jewish culture is the only possible godly culture.

3. How is Christ plus Moses a totally different gospel from Paul's?

The Galatians know their sins are forgiven, but they haven't "yet grappled enough with how potent the work of Christ was." They don't yet grasp "that this forgiveness was also sufficient to rescue them from 'the present evil age' [1:4]."[3] They've been rescued from the age when the lives of God's people had to be dictated by the law of Moses. The law itself was good, but it was given to expose how evil the unredeemed human heart is. And the age of freely following the Holy Spirit is so good that the age of the law was, by comparison, evil because it nullified the work of Christ.

4. Paul describes how passionately he used to practice Judaism (1:13 – 14). How then can he say the former age — when being an observant Jew was the best available life — was an "evil age"?

Why would such a life be especially bad for non-Jews like the Galatians?

GOING DEEPER

[I]f we distort the gospel in minimizing the centrality of Christ or the Spirit, we slip back into an age when Christ is not the rescuer and where the Spirit is not the one who brings us a life of freedom and love.[4]

5. Today we're unlikely to encounter distortions of the gospel that ask non-Jews to live like Jews. However, what are some false gospels that minimize the centrality of Christ or the Holy Spirit in other ways?

Heresies are appealing because they contain not total falsehood but distorted truth. They "are transformations of the real thing. In seeking for parallels in our current world we need to see what happens when the gospel is supplemented, augmented, altered, or changed."[5]

6. If a person claims faith in Christ, believes his sins are forgiven by grace, and shows no interest in growing in holiness or doing anything costly for the sake of Christ, how might the "gospel" he believes be a distortion of the true gospel of Christ?

7. If a person constantly tries to do the difficult things Jesus taught but struggles with feeling that she'll never measure up to God's standard, how might the "gospel" she believes be distorted?

8. If a person says Jesus Christ is the way he has found to experience God, but one could equally well find a path to God through practicing the law of Moses or the teachings of the Buddha, what would Paul say about that, and why?

9. How do you think we should deal with distortions of the gospel in our own churches or denominations?

The Judaizers' distorted gospel is often described in shorthand as legalism. It was legalism, but rules weren't the core of the problem. "[W]e must be on guard against the idea that every rule or regulation in Christian living is a necessary form of Galatian legalism. In fact, we are persuaded that rules can be educationally useful for Christian development. What we are looking for in applying the message of Galatians are rules or regulations that *distort* the gospel."[6]

In fact, most of the evangelical church today is in "a post-legalistic era."[7] The unnecessary social restrictions of the 1950s and before have largely been abandoned. Unfortunately, we haven't at the same time learned how to train Christians to listen to the Holy Spirit's guidance in ethics, which is the subject of Galatians 5–6.

10. How might rules be useful for Christian development without leading to legalism?

NOT FOR HUMAN APPROVAL[8]

Read Galatians 1:10, 15–24.

Paul's gospel was not based on human authority. It was also not shaped to win human approval. "[I]t can be inferred that the Judaizers had tried to convince the Galatians that Paul had trimmed his gospel to the bare essentials in order to court their approval — much like a computer salesperson who cuts all the 'bells and whistles' so as to make the system affordable to a penny-pinching customer. Paul counters: 'I am not trying to win your approval; I am preaching what God has revealed to me.' They respond back: 'Paul is preaching cheap grace, grace without law, acceptance by God without submission to God. Paul preaches a gospel that does not include the cost of Judaism and the law.'"[9]

11. When is it appropriate to seek human approval?

When is it not appropriate?

GOING DEEPER

[W]e need to guard our ideas and scope our practices to see if they are constructed in order to please people or if they have been constructed by people. We need to be constantly reforming our theology and our practices by checking each against the revelation of God in Christ and in his written Word.[10]

12. What has stood out to you from this discussion that you need to take to heart?

RESPONDING TO GOD'S WORD

IN YOUR GROUP:

In 1:13–24, Paul describes how the gospel of Jesus Christ transformed him. Your conversion might not have taken place in a dramatic moment like Paul's—maybe it took years, as Peter's did. (Was Peter converted in Luke 5? Mark 8? John 21? Acts 2?) But for both Peter and Paul their encounter with Christ, sudden or gradual, was what made sense of their life story.

Take three minutes to tell your group a piece of your life story that shows how your encounter with Christ has changed you. Tell about how you became a Christian, or tell one key turning point when Christ was pivotal. Is Christ what makes sense of your story? (If you're not yet a Christian, tell what drew you to this group.) Under "On Your Own" below are some questions. You could choose just one to answer in three minutes.

Depending on the size of your group, you may want to let half the group tell their stories in this session and let the other half do so in session 2. The group leader should plan ahead and go first. Don't aim for a blow-by-blow account of your whole life. Choose one key turning point. Do limit your story to three minutes. (It's a good idea to appoint a time keeper.) If you find this to be a beneficial activity, you can plan a whole meeting to share your stories.

End this time with prayers of thanksgiving:

> *Father, thank you for drawing each person here into your ongoing story. Thank you for revealing yourself to us and making us acceptable to you through your Son's death and resurrection. Help us to see you at work in our stories and to live according to the true gospel. In Jesus' name, amen.*

ON YOUR OWN:

Take an hour to start a first draft of your spiritual autobiography. Make a list of the key times in your life when Christ has played a central role in what you chose to do or in what happened to you. Here are some questions to get you started:

- Who was God to you when you were a child?
- When did Christ become more than just a name to you?

- How does Christ affect the work you spend most of your day doing?
- What have been the major turning points in your life? What role has Christ played in each of them?
- When have you been happy? How has (or hasn't) Christ affected that experience?
- When have you suffered significantly? How did (or didn't) Christ affect your response to suffering?

NOTES

1. This section is based on *NIVAC: Galatians*, 47–70.
2. McKnight, 48.
3. McKnight, 50.
4. McKnight, 57.
5. McKnight, 53.
6. McKnight, 53.
7. McKnight, 37.
8. This section is based on *NIVAC: Galatians*, 71–80.
9. McKnight, 63.
10. McKnight, 56.

RESISTING
PEER PRESSURE

Galatians 2:1–21

In China, the gospel is booming. Estimates of the number of Chinese Christians range from 54 million to 130 million — twenty to forty times the number of just thirty years ago. Much of the increase has come in urban churches which are Bible based, theologically conservative, and evangelical, but which do things that might surprise you. For instance, most of these new urban churches don't expect people to quit the Communist Party in order to join the church. In fact, they're happy to cooperate with the Communist government in social ministries. Their worship styles and other practices vary and can be very different from what Americans are used to.[1]

The gospel is on the move in China partly because leaders in these churches have grappled with the lessons of Galatians. They're asking, "What is the gospel?" and they're committed to spreading the gospel in its full and pure form — not, for instance, the gospel plus American culture. They know Chinese don't have to act like Americans in order to be fully Christian. There is one true gospel, but there are many cultural expressions of it.

For Jewish Christians in Paul's day, the idea that someone could be both a Gentile and a Christian was as hard to swallow as the idea that someone can be both a Communist and a Christian is for many Americans. Their Jewish heritage seemed as obviously essential to godliness as our democratic heritage can seem to us. But Paul stood his ground: Christ plus anything else, even something good, isn't the gospel.

TITUS: TEST CASE[2]

Read Galatians 2:1 – 10.

Paul said in Galatians 1 that he didn't receive his gospel from any human source, especially not from the apostles or the churches in and around Jerusalem. But while the leaders in Jerusalem weren't the *source* of his gospel, they did *approve* it when he laid it before them. Fourteen years after his conversion (probably two or three years before the writing of this letter), Paul presented his message to the Jerusalem-based apostles, and they gave him "the right hand of fellowship" (2:9) — public and formal approval. Paul even took along the Gentile Titus as a test case, and the apostles agreed that Titus was unmistakably Christian and didn't need to be circumcised (2:3). That is, he didn't need to become Jewish in order to be Christian.

1. List the key things the leaders or pillars of the Jerusalem church said and did in the meeting described in 2:1 – 10.

Why was the case of Titus significant?

Why did these decisions matter to the Galatians?

Some "false brothers" (Judaizers) were already at work at that meeting, raising the question of Titus's circumcision. Circumcision and kosher food laws were the key practices that set Jews apart from Gentiles. In describing the Judaizers' views, Paul uses the metaphor of "freedom" and "slaves" (2:4) that he'll expand upon later in this letter.

2. Why would it have been enslavement to compel Titus, a Gentile, to take on the practices that set Jews apart from Gentiles?

PETER: HYPOCRISY?[3]

Read Galatians 2:11 – 14.

Yet another incident with a Jerusalem leader illustrates why Paul's gospel is the correct one. In Jerusalem, Jews who didn't believe in Jesus were cracking down on Jews who did. Peter, one of Jesus' twelve apostles, even spent time in jail (Acts 12:1 – 19). He then went to Antioch in Syria (Gal. 2:11). This was probably not long after he approved Paul's ministry among Gentiles (2:9).

When Peter first went to Antioch, he had no problem eating Gentile food with Gentile converts. Gentile meat was a big taboo with the strict rabbis because some of it (such as pork and shellfish) was unclean according to Leviticus, and the rest of it was typically offered to a pagan god before being butchered. But Peter set aside this taboo for the sake of Christian unity—until some Judaizers arrived. They reminded him just how bad life could be for him and others back in Jerusalem if he kept carrying on this way, so he buckled under the pressure and stopped eating with the Gentiles.

Paul called Peter's behavior "hypocrisy" (2:13). In Jewish usage, the Greek word *hypocrites* didn't just mean being insincere or fake. It carried the sense of "wickedness, opposition to God and his truth, and even heresy."[4] That is, even Peter was behaving at times according to a false gospel (2:14).

3. What was it about Peter's actions that violated the gospel of God's acceptance through Christ?

4. The word "force" (2:14) is key here. How was Peter *forcing* Gentiles to seek acceptance through Jewish customs?

5. When do Christians today experience peer pressure to conform in ways that compromise the gospel?

PETER AND PAUL: JUSTIFICATION, FAITH, AND WORKS[5]

Read Galatians 2:15–21.

In the rest of this chapter, Paul describes what coming to grips with freedom in Christ means specifically for those who are "Jews by birth" (2:15). Gentiles don't have the disorienting experience of having lived their whole lives under the system of Moses, only to have Christ turn everything upside down.

Three terms in these crucial paragraphs—*justified*, *faith*, and *observing (works of) the law*—are key to understanding Galatians.

"*Justification* is a metaphor of our acceptance with God that is drawn from the world of law and jurisprudence."[6] We are guilty of violating God's good laws. We deserve punishment. God is altogether morally just, so he can't simply ignore our crimes. But through Christ's self-offering on the cross, God forgives us while at the same time serving justice. We are "justified"—our felony record is wiped clean so we can be reconciled with God.

6. What does Paul say in 2:15–21 about how a Jew is justified?

7. To be justified, one has to admit that one is guilty. But many people today lack a sense of guilt, because they don't think there are any absolute rights or wrongs. Something is right to them if it feels right, or if it produces desirable results. How would you help such a person come to believe they even need justification?

Faith begins with a mental agreement to certain facts: the crucifixion and resurrection of Christ and the salvation that comes through Christ. But for Paul, "it is also the continuing disposition of a Christian toward all that God has done in Christ (Rom. 1:17). We may thus define faith as *the initial and continual response of trust in, and obedience to, Christ by a person for the purpose of acceptance with God....* [W]hen Paul uses the term 'faith' (as in 'justified by faith'), he is describing both the initial act of trust and the continuing disposition of trust and obedience."[7]

8.   If we define faith as simply a mental agreement to certain facts, how does that affect the way we live as Christians?

If we define faith as mental agreement as well as a continual response of trust, surrender, and obedience, how does that affect the way we live as Christians?

How do you respond to this assertion that, for Paul, living by faith (2:20) includes ongoing obedience?

9. What then does it mean to be "justified" by "faith"?

The phrase "observing the law" (2:16) is literally "on the basis of the works of the law."[8] Paul is not talking in this verse about good works in the sense of "a lifestyle that is attractive, moral, and godly."[9] He thinks that sort of "good works" (Eph. 2:10) is an essential response of ongoing faith, and in Galatians he calls it "the fruit of the Spirit" (5:22–23).

The works Paul speaks against in 2:16 are works *of the law*—that is, conforming to the law of Moses in order to gain God's acceptance. He's against those works because they deny Christ's sufficiency and divide the Christian community along cultural lines. He's opposed to works of the law, but he's in favor of works of the Spirit.

10. How do you respond to this understanding of works? Does it make sense of Galatians 2:15–21 and the rest of Paul's writings? Or do you think it's incorrect? Please explain.

11. Jews have to "die to the law" (2:19)—they have to give up on the way of Moses as the means to God's acceptance. What are some things we today have to die to, or give up on, as means to God's acceptance?

12. How is the Holy Spirit calling you to respond to God's acceptance of you by faith in what Christ has done?

RESPONDING TO GOD'S WORD

IN YOUR GROUP:

If you didn't have time for everyone to tell their conversion or turning-point stories in session 1, let those who remain do so now.

If you did finish with your stories, then take time now for each person to share one current situation in which they need to live by faith in Christ. If your group is large, you might want to divide into subgroups of four for this. After each person shares, let the rest pray for them. If praying aloud in a group is new for some, they can say something as simple as:

> *Father, please send your Holy Spirit to enable _____ to trust and fully surrender to you in this situation, taking the action you are calling them to take. In Jesus' name, amen.*

ON YOUR OWN:

Keep working on your spiritual autobiography. Write down three situations when being justified by faith in Christ has affected your choices — or when it could have but didn't. Then step back and look at the pattern. Are you a person who struggles with guilt and has difficulty acting in the knowledge that God fully accepts you? Or are you someone who tends to be complacent, taking your salvation for granted and not giving much thought to what God wants you to do in response? Has justification made you braver, more loving, more at peace with yourself and others? Or has it made you a diligent church-goer but not a more loving person?

NOTES

1. Rob Moll, "Great Leap Forward," *Christianity Today*, May 2008, 26.
2. This section is based on *NIVAC: Galatians*, 81–98.
3. This section is based on *NIVAC: Galatians*, 99–114.
4. McKnight, 106.
5. This section is based on *NIVAC: Galatians*, 115–134.
6. McKnight, 119.
7. McKnight, 121–122, italics original.
8. McKnight, 119.
9. McKnight, 121.

TYPEWRITERS IN THE COMPUTER AGE

Galatians 3:1–25

By the early twentieth century, the mechanical typewriter was starting to revolutionize communications. Many great novelists continued to write by hand, but for lawyers, businesspeople, journalists, and others, the typewriter was a blessing.

As excellent as the typewriter was, though, we have to wonder about people who continue to use their IBM Selectrics in the twenty-first century when the personal computer is available and affordable. "Everything that a typewriter wanted to be when it was a little boy (and more!) is now found in the computer."[1] Computer keyboards and word processing programs depend on the technology of typewriters, yet they transcend typewriters. "When the computer age arrived, we put away our manual typewriters because they belonged to the former era.... But in putting them away, we do not destroy them. We fulfill them.... Every maneuver on a computer is the final hope of the manual typewriter."[2]

The relationship of the typewriter age to the computer age is like the relationship Paul sees between the era of the law and the era of Christ and the Spirit. The law was a crucial step in God's plan of salvation. When God gave the law to Moses, it took the Israelites light years deeper into God's will. But its purpose was temporary and limited, and now Christ has both fulfilled and surpassed it. Those who live by faith in Christ through the Spirit fulfill what the law pointed toward. So asking a Gentile Christian to adopt the law of Moses is like making her use an old typewriter when she could have a laptop.

ARGUMENT FROM EXPERIENCE[3]

Read Galatians 3:1–5.

In explaining his views on the law of Moses versus Christ, Paul now appeals to the Galatians' experience with a series of rhetorical questions. He doesn't answer the questions because he thinks the answers are obvious.

1. What answers do you think are supposed to come to mind when the Galatians read each of Paul's questions in 3:2–5?

Central to Paul's point here is that the Galatians received the Holy Spirit long before they were asked to keep the law.

GOING DEEPER

For Paul, receiving the Spirit is the identifying characteristic of the Christian. To be a Christian is to be indwelt by the Spirit, and to be indwelt by the Spirit is to be a Christian (cf. Rom. 8:9–11).... Paul says that the Christian's very beginning is with the Spirit (v. 3), and he contends that God works among Christians through the Spirit (v. 5). Faith brings the blessing of Abraham, and this blessing is the "promise of the Spirit" (v. 14). Later, he says that those who are truly sons of God are those who have been granted the Spirit, who calls out "Abba, Father" (4:6).

What Paul is talking about here may be an experience, and it may very well be a charismatic one, but it is not some experience subsequent to faith in Christ. For Paul, faith in Christ means being granted God's Spirit. This granting of the Spirit ends the age of the law.[4]

2. Some Christians believe that after we put our faith in Christ, we need to pray to receive the Holy Spirit as an additional experience. As you read Paul, what are the arguments for or against this view?

If receiving the Holy Spirit is an essential part of being a Christian, what are the implications for us today?

3. Paul points to receiving the Spirit as a memorable experience for the Galatians. He even mentions miracles (3:5). Should we expect that receiving the Spirit will be a memorable experience today? What should we expect, and why?

What has been your experience of the Holy Spirit?

In 3:3, the TNIV reads "trying to finish by human effort." The original wording is "trying to finish by flesh." The issue isn't lack of effort (faith) versus effort (to earn God's approval). Rather, to live "by flesh" means to rely on something other than Christ's work and the power of the Spirit. Living by the Spirit does involve effort. It doesn't involve merit-seeking, or cultural add-ons like circumcision, or sheer willpower without the Spirit's help.

4. Describe some of the efforts it takes to live by the Spirit.

ARGUMENT FROM SCRIPTURE[5]

Read Galatians 3:6–18.

The books of Moses themselves support Paul's views about the law. Jews saw Abraham as "the quintessential Jew"[6] but Abraham lived centuries before God gave the law to Moses. And so whatever Abraham was, he was not a keeper of the law of Moses. In Genesis 15:6 (quoted in Gal. 3:6) God declares Abraham righteous (justified) because of his faith, and in Genesis 12:3; 18:18; 22:18 (quoted in Gal. 3:8) God repeatedly promises that the nations (Gentiles) and not just the Jews would be blessed through Abraham.

5. Why does it matter to the Galatians that justification by faith and salvation for the Gentiles were always the plan, even back in Abraham's day?

6. Was Abraham's "faith" a matter simply of believing true things about God, or did it involve a surrender of his whole life to God's purposes? Explain your reasoning. (Some relevant passages are Genesis 12:1–5; 15:1–6; 17:1–2; 22:1–18.)

Those Jews who base their hopes of salvation on the law must face the curses declared in that same law. The law was never meant *"to make someone righteous"* or *"to give salvation or life"*[7] (see 3:21). It was always meant to make humans aware of their sinful compulsions and make them put their trust in God's provision. To illustrate how deeply humans needed something done about their sin, the law told them to continually confess sin and shed the blood of animals for atonement.

GOING DEEPER

The term *redeemed* is drawn from the commercial world and describes "purchasing things," "buying back a captive," "liberating a slave through a ransom payment," or "securing the interests of a family by offering a fee."[8]

7. What then does it mean to say that Christ "redeemed" Jews from the curse of the law (3:13)?

8. How did Christ "become a curse" (3:13)?

In 3:15–18, Paul talks about God's covenant (agreement) with Abraham. *"[W]hat Paul is doing with the Galatians is teaching them how to read the Bible properly....* They had learned to read the Bible through the eyes of Moses as interpreted by the priests and Pharisees; Paul wants them to learn to read the Bible through the eyes of Abraham."[9] These two ways of reading the Old Testament can be compared like this:

Abraham	Moses
Covenant based on promise	Covenant based on law-keeping
Faith is the response to God's offer of a covenant	Keeping the law is the response to God's offer of a covenant
Emphasis on God's plan for all the nations (Gen. 12:2–3)	Nationalistic emphasis on Israel

9. For Paul, it's crucial to read the Bible in its historical context. The story of Abraham in Genesis helps us understand what's going on in the story of Moses, in the books of the prophets, and in the life of Jesus. How does this compare to the way you typically read the Bible?

How does it compare to the way the Bible is handled in your church?

THE PURPOSE OF THE LAW[10]

Read Galatians 3:19–25.

From what Paul has said, you could get the impression that the law was pointless. So he clarifies: The law did have a valuable purpose. "It was added because of transgressions" (3:19), that is, for the purpose of revealing what transgressions are.

10. How does the law reveal certain kinds of behavior as sinful?

Despite this valuable purpose, though, the law had limited shelf life: "It was added [after the covenant with Abraham] ... until the Seed to whom the promise referred had come" (3:19). The law couldn't give people righteousness or eternal life (3:21); instead it declared them guilty and held them in custody (3:22–25) until the promise was fulfilled and the era of faith in Christ arrived. (Several times in this passage Paul uses the Greek word *paidagogos*, or "pedagogue," which in this context means something that governed the Jews until Christ came.)

11. Paul says that because of the Jews' sin, the law held them in custody until Christ/faith came to redeem/free them. What attitudes toward the law do you think Paul wants the Gentile Galatians to have?

Christians live in faith by the Spirit rather than under the law, but that doesn't mean Paul wants us to rip the books of Moses out of our Bibles and throw them away. The law is still useful to us as:

- "a preliminary sketch of God's moral will"[11]
- the foundation of Christian ethics to the extent that the law underlies what Jesus and the apostles teach in the New Testament
- a force that reveals human sin

12. Look at Leviticus 19 (for example) and talk about how this passage of the law can be useful today in these three ways.

GOING DEEPER

Christians who are seeking God's will do not turn first of all to the law of Moses for direction. Instead, they listen to God's Spirit and to the teachings of Jesus ("the law of Christ"; see 6:2); both of these teach them that they are to "love God" and "love others." In following the Spirit and Christ, the Christian will always do what the law tried to tell them... to do. Thus, they will actually do God's will.[12]

13. Is the New Testament our "law" in the age of Christ? Is following the Spirit simply a matter of asking what the New Testament says? Explain your view.

In sessions 5 and 6 we will explore how one follows the Spirit's guidance.

RESPONDING TO GOD'S WORD

IN YOUR GROUP:

Galatians 3 begins with the Galatians' personal experience of the Holy Spirit. In response, take a minute or two to talk about your experience of the Holy Spirit. Your experience may not be flashy but might involve the Spirit convicting you of sin, encouraging you about God's forgiveness, guiding you, or transforming you. When have you found yourself able to surrender the whole of yourself to what God was doing and sign on to serve him despite the cost? The Spirit was certainly involved then.

After everyone has shared, thank God for the Spirit's activity in your lives:

Father, thank you for sending your Holy Spirit to convict, encourage, strengthen, guide, and transform us. Thank you for the times he works silently as well as the times he works dramatically. Help us to hear and respond to him. In Jesus' name, amen.

ON YOUR OWN:

Add the Holy Spirit to your spiritual autobiography. When has he been active in your life, and how? Looking back, where do you see him convicting, encouraging, strengthening, guiding, or transforming you? If he seems invisible in your story, write a list of questions you have about him. Then ask him to guide you to answers.

NOTES

1. McKnight, *NIVAC: Galatians*, 184.
2. Ibid.
3. This section is based on *NIVAC: Galatians*, 135–148.
4. McKnight, 138.
5. This section is based on *NIVAC: Galatians*, 149–175.
6. McKnight, 151.
7. McKnight, 155, italics original.
8. McKnight, 156, italics original.
9. McKnight, 166, italics original.
10. This section is based on *NIVAC: Galatians*, 176–194.
11. McKnight, 186.
12. McKnight, 188, italics original.

NO LONGER SLAVES

Galatians 3:26 – 4:31

Teenagers are acutely aware of our culture's privileges of adulthood. One gets a driver's license at a certain age, and some states set a later age when passenger restrictions cease. Because we have a drinking age, many young people view their first drink as a rite of passage. Many look forward to the day when they will no longer have a curfew, no longer have to check in with a parent about where they're going and with whom.

Adults know there are good reasons for placing limits on what underage people can do. Adults also know that adulthood brings responsibilities as well as privileges. Still, most adults are glad that the time of being looked after and constantly corrected is past.

This is the sense of relief and freedom Paul feels when he thinks about being one of God's adult children. He has a Father to whom he continues to call out, "Abba!" with affection and respect. But he's not a child with a nanny; he's an adult son and heir.

SONS (AND DAUGHTERS) OF GOD[1]

Read Galatians 3:26 – 4:7.

Paul's theme in this passage is *sonship:* By faith the Galatians have already become God's sons and, consequently, heirs.

Recent translations have moved away from calling us "sons of God" and toward calling us "children of God" in order to make it clear that manliness is the last thing on Paul's mind. However, the point of "sons" is that in Paul's day, daughters didn't inherit their fathers' property or rights. They spent their whole lives under guardians. But in God's family all Christians, both male and female (3:28), have the rights that Roman law gave to adult sons. We don't need the law as our guardian, because we're adults, heirs of God our Father.

A "son of God" is one who has been set free from tutelage and turned loose with God's Spirit to guide them.[2]

GOING DEEPER

1. Paul repeats the word "all" in 3:26, 27, and 28. What is the significance of this word "all"?

By emphasizing "all," does Paul mean that all humans will eventually enjoy eternal life? Please explain.

[A] "son of God" is one who learns to call God *Abba* because God has given his Spirit to his sons. Calling God *Abba* is the most intimate language of the family in the Jewish world. This was the first term a Jewish child learned (along with *imma*, 'mommy'), and it can be translated "daddy." While "daddy" is accurate, there is more to it than the language of a child. The father, the *abba*, in Judaism was also a

GOING DEEPER

commanding authority figure for the Jewish family, and children were taught never to disagree with and always to honor him. Thus, the term *abba* is not just the prattling of a child, not just the language of little children with their loving fathers playing games and talking sweet things; rather, it is the term that Jews used for their relationship to their fathers that involved both relational intimacy and honorable respect.[3]

2. How do we develop intimacy with and respect for God, our Abba?

Christians have been "baptized into Christ" (3:27) and are now "in Christ Jesus" (3:26, 28). That is, "Christians have been swallowed up into Christ so that they live in him and out of a relationship to him. To be 'in Christ' is to be in spiritual fellowship with him through God's Spirit."[4]

3. Being "in Christ Jesus" is more significant for your identity than what you do for a living, what ethnic group or nation you belong to, what social class you're in, how much money you make, what church you attend, or whether you're male or female. If this is so, then what are the implications for the choices you make and the way you respond to life?

4. Do you believe God means for there to be "black churches," "white churches," "Hispanic churches," etc.? If so, why? If not, why not?

How has white American culture affected the gospel that is preached and practiced in white American churches?

5. Paul speaks of God as Father, Son, and Holy Spirit. In 4:6, how do these three persons of the one God interact with one another?

PAUL THE PASTOR[5]

Read Galatians 4:8–20.

In 4:3, Paul said Jews under the law were enslaved under "the elemental spiritual forces of the world." That is, the law was "the 'ABCs' of God's revelation."[6] The Gentile Galatians were formerly enslaved to pagan gods (4:8), which were "weak and miserable forces" (4:9) essentially like those that enslaved the Jews. To equate Jewish religion with pagan religion would have mortally offended the Judaizers. But "[e]very human being, Paul would say, is captive to the 'elemental principles' in some way and is only set free by Jesus Christ."[7]

6. Paul has been laying out his case with Scripture and logic, but in 4:8–20 he expresses his emotions. What are some of his emotional statements in this passage?

What emotions is Paul feeling?

Why does he feel so passionately about this situation?

"Zeal" is a key term in 4:17–18. Paul is passionate or zealous in a positive sense, but "used negatively, this term describes an emotion of 'jealousy' and 'intensity' that seeks to remedy a situation, frequently with violence." In Jerusalem there was a Zealot party (see Matt. 10:4), and by AD 66 their "sole ambition, through use of violence, was to defeat Rome and establish Jerusalem as the place that worshiped one God."[8]

We don't know if the Judaizers were violent Zealots with a political agenda, but we know they were nationalists and used at least social pressure (2:12) to "compel" (6:12) converts to join their nationalist agenda.

7. Are you zealous about anything, in a good or bad sense? If so, about what, and how? If not, how do you view those who are zealous?

8. Paul is zealous about seeing Christ formed in his readers (4:19). What does it mean for Christ to be formed in a person? (See, for example, Gal. 2:20; Rom. 12:1–2; 2 Cor. 3:18; Eph. 4:23–24.)

9. Paul says "become like me" (4:12). How passionate are you about Christ being formed in yourself? In those around you? Why is that?

ABRAHAM'S TWO SONS[9]

Read Galatians 4:21–31.

Once again Paul reads the Old Testament through the lens of Christ. The Judaizers claim that the Jews are the heirs of the promise because they are the descendants of Isaac. But Paul turns that argument on its head by making the story of Abraham's two sons foreshadow Christ.

Law	Christ
Abraham	
Hagar Covenant	Sarah Covenant
Ishmael ("flesh")	Isaac ("promise")
Persecutor	Persecuted
Children—Slaves	Children—Free ones
Mount Sinai	(Mount Zion? Golgotha? Heaven?)
Earthly Jerusalem in slavery	Heavenly Jerusalem in freedom
Judaizers	**Paul**
Old Covenant	**New Covenant**

It may appear here that Paul is setting aside the original meaning of the story of Abraham, Sarah, and Hagar for it is not obvious how he reaches such a radical conclusion that the Judaizers are not the true descendents of Abraham. However, biblical scholarship has shown that Paul's argument flows logically from how the book of Isaiah uses the story of Abraham and Sarah in its prophecies when those prophecies are understood in light of the resurrection of Jesus Christ.

10. What aspects of 4:21–31 might offend a Jewish person who didn't believe in Christ?

11. Throughout this chapter, the themes of slavery and freedom recur. What, for Paul, does slavery, or childhood, refer to?

What is freedom, or adulthood?

12. How can you live more fully as a son (an adult child with full rights) of God?

RESPONDING TO GOD'S WORD

IN YOUR GROUP:

Calling God "Abba" raises the complex feelings we have toward our natural fathers. If your group is large, divide into subgroups of four. Give each person a chance to finish this sentence: "When I think of calling God 'Abba,' I _____."

After everyone has done this, pray for each person along these lines:

Abba, we love you and we stand in awe of you. Thank you for giving us the privilege of calling you Abba. [Name] feels [nervous, grateful, ambivalent, joyful, resistant, sad, etc.] calling you that because _____, so please help him/her to know you more fully as Abba. Amen.

ON YOUR OWN:

Where do your natural parents fit into your spiritual autobiography? Maybe they raised you in faith. Maybe they had no faith or a faith different from what you now believe. Probably they have influenced what goes through your mind when you call God "Abba, Father." Add your parents to your spiritual autobiography.

If you have time, also think about how your view of God as Father has changed, or not changed, over the years. If you called him Father when you were ten, how is it the same or different for you now? Add that development to your autobiography.

NOTES

1. This section is based on *NIVAC: Galatians*, 195–214.
2. McKnight, 213.
3. McKnight, 212.
4. McKnight, 199.
5. This section is based on *NIVAC: Galatians*, 215–226.
6. McKnight, 204.
7. McKnight, 217.
8. McKnight, 220.
9. This section is based on *NIVAC: Galatians*, 227–241.

TRUE FREEDOM

Galatians 5:1–26

The transition to adulthood spells new freedoms, but in our society freedom is often defined in self-centered and self-indulgent terms. Adults are free to drink as much as they want and to stay out all night wherever they please. They may claim absolute control over their lives ("as long as it doesn't hurt anybody else"). In this view, neither the government, nor others in the community, nor a spouse, nor the church, nor God has the right to limit a person's autonomy. Each adult is his or her own sovereign. One's primary responsibility is to define and fully express one's self.

This is far from how Paul defines freedom. He has a different view of what we're free *from* and what we're free *for*. The Judaizers think that without the law Christians will behave selfishly, like out-of-control college students on a spring break party spree. But Paul says Christians who truly are Christians — who live freely in Christ and follow the Holy Spirit — won't do that. In fact, he argues, they'll be more holy and loving than those who remain enslaved to the law.

FAITH EXPRESSED THROUGH LOVE[1]

Read Galatians 5:1 – 12.

Paul insists that life under the law is a kind of slavery, while the life of faith is freedom. By "freedom" he means:

FREE HOW?

- Free "as a result of Christ's death" (not because freedom is a right we're born with)[2]
- Free "as a work of God in our lives through Christ Jesus and the Holy Spirit" (not because we make it happen, or because life owes us freedom)[3]

FREE FROM WHAT?

- Free from the curse that the law pronounces on sinners (not free from the discomfort of facing our sinfulness)
- "Free from everything that shackles [us] to sin and ugliness" (not free from feeling bad when we do sinful, ugly things)[4]
- Free from self-centeredness
- Free from social barriers that divide people and hinder love (3:28)
- Not free from responsibility to anybody else, whether God or other people
- Not free from the call to love
- Not free from the need to act in faith daily

FREE FOR WHAT?

- Free for relationship with God (not free to be self-sufficient, independent individuals)
- Free to live life in the Spirit of God (not free for life according to our agenda and by our will)
- Free to be who God wants us to be (not free to be the person we fantasize about being, the self we invent)
- Free to do what God wants us to do (not free to do whatever we want)
- Free to love God with our whole being
- Free to become selflessly loving toward other people (not free to put our own desires first; 5:6, 19 – 23)

1. Based on what you've read in Galatians and elsewhere in the New Testament, respond to the above definition of freedom. In what ways do you agree or disagree that this is the freedom Paul is talking about in 5:1?

    In what ways do you find this a good or flawed definition of the freedom we should seek?

    How is this definition of freedom like and unlike the freedom promoted in our culture (in the political sphere, on television, and so on)?

2. Another aspect of freedom that is much discussed today is "the breaking down of social structures that are perceived to be oppressive or obstacles to equality and justice."[5] What place does this kind of freedom have in the freedom Paul calls for?

3. Paul says "Christ will be of no value to you" (5:2) if you opt for the law's system, because that means opting out of the Christ/grace system. Why can't a person follow Christ *and* treat the law as an essential part of the Christian life?

Paul even says that seeking justification through the law equals being "alienated from Christ" and "fallen away from grace" (5:4). Is he saying that a believer can lose his salvation? In brief, we "believe the overall teaching of the New Testament assumes that Christians will persevere; there are numerous utterances of the assurance that they can have of their final destiny. [Yet] there are enough 'terrifying' passages to make one think apostasy is a real possibility and that in the case of apostasy one can 'forfeit one's salvation.' "[6]

Apostasy is intentionally, even gleefully and violently, denouncing one's relationship to Christ and refusing to submit to God's will. It can't be done accidentally, so nobody who worries about doing it has done it.

4. In 5:5 Paul says "by faith we eagerly await through the Spirit the righteousness [same word family as "justified" in 5:4] for which we hope." In what sense do we already possess righteousness?

In what sense is righteousness something we eagerly await by faith?

5. According to Paul, the only thing that counts with God is "faith expressing itself through love" (5:6). If faith is just agreement with a set of doctrines and doesn't express itself through love, can it still be the kind of faith that brings salvation? Please explain your view.

WALK BY THE SPIRIT[7]

Read Galatians 5:13–26.

Just as living under the law is a kind of slavery, so living under sin—the tyranny of one's desires—is slavery. The "sinful nature" (in some translations "flesh"; 5:13, 16, 17, 19) isn't the body, but rather the total person, both body and soul, "living outside of God's will and apart from God's guiding influence through the Spirit."[8] The Judaizers think the Holy Spirit in a Christian's life isn't enough to overcome the temptations of the "flesh," such as sexual sin and idolatry. But Paul says the whole law-system is fleshly, because it evades God's Spirit.

6. Why is freedom for self-indulgence actually slavery?

GOING DEEPER

Legalists are led by the law; hedonists are led by their desires; materialists are led by their possessions. But sons of God, Christians, are led by the Spirit. What prompts their actions, what stirs their emotions, what guides their behavior, and what determines their careers is God's Spirit. Furthermore, sons of God do not fear and worry about where the Spirit will lead them. They know that God's Spirit will lead them perfectly into God's will and God's blessing so they march behind confidently and joyously."[9]

7. What does it mean in the practical terms of daily life to "walk by the Spirit" (5:16)?

How does the Spirit guide us, and how do we listen to him?

The Christian life "is life in the Spirit, the life of a person who is surrendered to letting the Spirit have complete control.... [O]ne does not gain this life by discipline or by mustering up the energy. One does not huddle with oneself in the morning, gather together his or her forces, and charge onto the field of life full of self-determined direction. Rather, the Christian life is a life of consistent surrender to the Spirit."[10]

8. Do you believe walking by the Spirit is enough to keep Christians out of sin, or do you think Christians need some system of rules too? Explain.

For Paul, the love that sums up the whole law is *defined* by Christ's sacrificial giving of his life in love (2:20), is *inspired* by God's Spirit (5:22–23), and is *expressed* in doing good and in interpersonal relationships in society, especially the church (5:13–14; 6:10).[11]

9. Love is "fruit," something the Spirit enables us to do (5:22). How does the Spirit enable us to love as Christ did?

10. Paul also says we have our part to do in bearing this fruit: We choose to "walk by the Spirit" (5:16) and "keep in step with the Spirit" (5:25). True saving faith in Christ crucifies the sinful nature "with its passions and desires" (5:24). What do we do when one of those fleshly desires arises in our mind?

Other than sexual sin, drunkenness, and idolatry, the fleshly behaviors Paul warns against in this passage have to do with fights between groups: "biting and devouring each other" (5:15), "discord, jealousy, fits of rage, selfish ambition, dissensions, factions and envy" (5:20–21). He focuses on these probably because the Galatians have divided into hostile factions—the pro-Paul faction and the pro-circumcision faction—with rivalries that broke fellowship between house churches.[12]

Likewise, the fruit of the Spirit in 5:22–23 focuses on interpersonal relations, because that's the issue at hand. This isn't an exhaustive list of everything the Spirit works to produce in us. (One could add holiness and justice, for example.)

11. To be a Christian is to have the Spirit through faith in Christ (4:6) and to choose to walk in the Spirit rather than in the sinful nature (5:5–6, 16–17). Why, then, are the acts of the sinful nature (particularly "discord,

jealousy, fits of rage," etc.) so common in churches—even among people who have accurate beliefs about Jesus?

12. What will walking in the Spirit rather than the sinful nature mean doing differently for you this week?

RESPONDING TO GOD'S WORD

IN YOUR GROUP:

One essential part of walking in the Spirit is being frankly honest before God about ourselves. The Bible calls this "confession." Until we face up to who we really are (sinful, imperfect people who live in the constant pain of our imperfection), we cannot be free. This is not a "solidarity confession" (I, with everyone else, am a sinner) but a "solitary confession" (I, though no else be with me, am a sinner). When we come to God on his terms, admitting who we truly are, we will gain access to his freedom.[13]

Depending on the trust level in your group, it might be good to focus your prayers on confession. In most groups detailing your sexual sins won't be appropriate, but you might consider separating into subgroups—one for men and one for women—to offer even one sin to God in the presence of fellow believers. You envy someone. You loathe someone at work. You have trouble controlling your temper with your kids. Pick something you genuinely struggle with, something you feel you can trust this group to know about (is confidentiality a ground rule in your group?), and offer it to God in prayer. Then pray for each other:

> *Father, by faith in Christ we have crucified our sinful nature with its harmful desires, but we find some of those desires are still embedded in our habits of mind. Please forgive us for the things we have confessed and, by your Spirit, change our thinking and our doing. By your Spirit, help us hate these sins, to strengthen us to say no to them, to fill our minds with thoughts that please you, to guide us in whatever action you want us to take. Thank you for freeing us in Christ from the guilt of these sins, and for freeing us in the Spirit from continuing to practice them. Amen.*

ON YOUR OWN:

You can take confession deeper on your own. God already knows everything we do and think, but when we list them for him we are acknowledging our sin. Tell God the acts of the sinful nature (mind as well as body) that are habits for you. You might find it helpful to write your confession or speak it aloud. It's normal to feel some shame when you do this, but if you're flooded with feelings of shame, and meditating on God's forgiveness doesn't help, you might want to talk to your pastor or another mature Christian about this.

NOTES

1. This section is based on *NIVAC: Galatians*, 242–261.
2. McKnight, 244.
3. Ibid.
4. McKnight, 245.
5. McKnight, 255.
6. McKnight, 250.
7. This section is based on *NIVAC: Galatians*, 262–281.
8. McKnight, 266, quoting R. N. Longenecker, *Galatians*, Word Biblical Commentary vol. 41 (Dallas: Word, 1990), 239–41.
9. McKnight, 213–214.
10. McKnight, 269.
11. McKnight, 267–268.
12. McKnight, 267.
13. McKnight, 259.

A COMMUNITY GUIDED BY THE SPIRIT

Galatians 6:1–18

M any people today are drawn to Jesus but repelled by the church. Churches are full of exactly the discord and jealousy Paul rebuked in Galatians 5, so it seems sensible to many people to avoid churches and manage their lives in the Spirit on their own, or perhaps with a loose network of friends. Friends can be dropped if they get burdensome.

But Dietrich Bonhoeffer, a German pastor and teacher who spent two years in concentration camps before the Nazis finally executed him, made an astonishing claim in his book *Life Together:* God intends that churches disillusion us. "The serious Christian, set down for the first time in a Christian community, is likely to bring with him a very definite idea of what Christian life together should be and to try to realize it. But God's grace speedily shatters such dreams."[1]

God wants us to learn to love real people, not ideal people. He wants to train us to love the kind of people who are too annoying for our sinful nature to love, people we can love only in the power of the Spirit. That's real Christian community, and it's the kind of life in the Spirit to which Paul calls the Galatians in his final words.

MUTUALLY ACCOUNTABLE AND PERSONALLY RESPONSIBLE[2]

Read Galatians 6:1 – 10.

The Galatians have split into at least two factions — one that is pro-law/circumcision and one that is anti-law/circumcision. Cruel words and maybe actions have gone back and forth. But now, perhaps those who have refused to be circumcised feel smug as they hear Paul's letter: They are right and their ex-friends are wrong! Perhaps some of those who have given in to the pressure to be circumcised are overcome with shame as they read Paul's letter. They may even be terrified that they've lost God's grace forever, perhaps having committed an unforgivable sin. They can't imagine crawling back to those in the other camp who will humiliate them. Paul foresees these feelings, so he coaches all of these people on how to live together now.

1. In 6:1 – 5, what is Paul's counsel to those who are "spiritual," who are living in the Spirit and have to respond to those who have sinned?

2. "Gently" in 6:1 is literally, "in the spirit of gentleness." It recalls 5:23, where Paul said gentleness was a fruit of the Spirit. Why is gentleness so important when we're dealing with someone who has admitted his sin?

3. The spiritual may not be tempted to do what the sinner did, but they may well be tempted by arrogance, which is an equally dangerous sin. How does Paul deflate their arrogance?

Paul asserts that Christians are accountable to one another — they must "carry each other's burdens" (6:2). That is, they must "not only ... point out [another person's] problems and sins, but also ... carry the responsibility of helping that person become free of that entanglement."[3]

4. How do you respond to the idea of being that involved in other people's lives, and having other people that involved in yours?

The "law of Christ" is "(1) submission to the teachings of Jesus that fulfill the law (Matt. 5:17–20) and (2) life in the Spirit, which is essentially love and which itself fulfills the law of Moses (Gal. 5:6, 14, 18, 22). The Christian's law is following Jesus, that is, living in submission to the Spirit."[4] After all, it was the same Spirit who inspired the law of Moses in the first place.

5. While Christians are mutually accountable to one another, each person is also directly responsible to God for his or her own actions. How does Paul describe our personal accountability to God in 6:4–5, 7–9?

God is the Judge, and people cannot sneer at him.... If a person lives to the flesh, that person will "reap destruction" (condemnation); if a person lives "in the Spirit," that person will "reap eternal life." What Paul is saying is ... while works do not save us, no one is saved without works. Why? Very simply, because works are the sure indicators of a person's heart, orientation, and status before God. Every judgment in the Bible is a judgment according to works (cf. Matt. 7:13–27; 16:27; 22:1–14; 25:1–46; 2 Cor. 5:10; Rev. 20:11–15). A person's final standing before God will be determined by that person's relationship to Jesus Christ as revealed in his or her works. While it is absolutely true that our grounds of acceptance is the sacrifice Jesus Christ made on our behalf, our connection to that sacrifice is by way of a faith that works itself out in the many good works in a person's life.[5]

6. What do you think about this idea that a person's faith in Jesus Christ is revealed by his or her works, so we will be judged by our works? Does it sound consistent with what Paul has said earlier?

If this is true, what are the implications for you? If it's not true, what are the implications?

7. What if a person was abused as a child or has a genetic predisposition to alcoholism? How do genes or past experiences affect our personal responsibility for our adult behavior, if at all?

FINAL WORDS IN BIG LETTERS[6]

Read Galatians 6:11 – 18.

"It was customary for ancient authors to use a secretary because they were trained to write quickly, neatly, and in limited space."[7] But now Paul takes the pen from his secretary (called an amanuensis) and summarizes his main points in his own handwriting.

He has several problems with the Judaizers. The first is that they are "trying to compel" (6:12) the Galatians to obey them — through psychological pressure ("You're not really saved if you don't do this!") if not physical.

8. Have you ever seen psychological pressure used in the church to make people conform? If so, when?

Another problem with the Judaizers was that their motive was fear: "to avoid being persecuted for the cross of Christ" (6:12) by fellow Jews.

9. Have you ever seen people go along with pressuring someone else to conform because they were afraid of what would happen if they didn't? If so, when?

Also, the Judaizers' goal was "to boast about" getting as many converts as possible (6:13), which amounts to "mere scalp-hunting."[8] Church leaders and missionaries often feel enormous pressure to hit numerical targets: How many people attended this Sunday? How many prayed the prayer to receive Christ? How many were baptized this year? How many tithed?

10. Paul refuses to boast about numbers, because he's been crucified to all that sort of thing that impresses the world (6:14). What do you think it means to boast only in the cross of Christ?

What are the potential costs of doing this?

What counts for Paul is "the new creation" (6:15). In the Western world this is frequently understood in exclusively individualistic terms. While it's true that the individual Christian is a new creation, Paul's main thought here is that God's new people is a new creation—a family where anyone can belong by faith, regardless of race, nationality, class, income, or gender.

11. As you look back at this study of Galatians, what is the Holy Spirit asking you to remember and live by?

12. How can you participate more fully in the "new creation" God has made?

RESPONDING TO GOD'S WORD

IN YOUR GROUP:

The end of a study is a good time to celebrate. Share some extra food and drink, and talk about what you've gained from this group. Some music that celebrates the Holy Spirit would be fitting. Here is a hymn by Bianco of Siena (who died in 1434), translated from Italian to English by Richard F. Littledale in *The People's Hymnal*, 1867:

Come down, O love divine, seek Thou this soul of mine,
And visit it with Thine own ardor glowing.
O Comforter, draw near, within my heart appear,
And kindle it, Thy holy flame bestowing.

O let it freely burn, till earthly passions turn
To dust and ashes in its heat consuming;
And let Thy glorious light shine ever on my sight,
And clothe me round, the while my path illuming.

And so the yearning strong, with which the soul will long,
Shall far outpass the power of human telling;
For none can guess its grace, till he become the place
Wherein the Holy Spirit makes His dwelling.

ON YOUR OWN:

Pray about mutual accountability and personal responsibility. In your life as a Christian up to now, when have you taken personal responsibility for your actions, and when perhaps have you avoided it? Think of at least one situation that was a high or low point on this theme, and write about it.

Next, in your life as a Christian up to now, when have you been mutually accountable with other Christians, and when perhaps have you chosen not to let people too far inside your life? Think of at least one situation that was a high or low point on this theme, and write about it.

What about now? Is the Spirit calling you to more mutual accountability? If so, what can you do? What is the Spirit saying to you about personal responsibility?

NOTES

1. Dietrich Bonhoeffer, *Life Together* (New York: Harper and Row, 1954), 26.
2. This section is based on *NIVAC: Galatians*, 282–296.
3. McKnight, 285.
4. Ibid.
5. McKnight, 287.
6. This section is based on *NIVAC: Galatians*, 297–311.
7. McKnight, 299.
8. McKnight, 300, quoting F. F. Bruce, *The Epistle to the Galatians*, New International Greek Testament Commentary (Grand Rapids: Eerdmans, 1982), 270.

LEADER'S NOTES

SESSION 1 LEADER'S NOTES

This study of the book of Galatians focuses on the sufficiency of Jesus Christ and the Holy Spirit, both in bringing us to salvation and in guiding us through the Christian life. In Galatians, Paul alternates between reasoning from Scripture and talking about personal experiences — his own and the Galatians'. The discussion questions throughout this guide emphasize reasoning, while the "Responding to God's Word" section at the end of each session invites your group to tell each other stories of how you came to Christ and how you live in Christ. Telling personal stories deepens intimacy in a group, and reflecting on your own and others' experiences in light of Scripture will help you see what the Spirit has been doing.

1. Paul wants his readers to know that his gospel came from God and doesn't need to be supplemented by the teaching the Judaizers offer. He appeals to his dramatic conversion experience as persuasive evidence. Later he'll buttress his claim by showing that the rest of Scripture (at that time there was only the Old Testament) is consistent with his gospel and not with the teaching of the Judaizers. He'll also show that while the Jerusalem apostles weren't the source of his teaching, they did endorse it and him.

    Today we are right to reject anybody who claims authority to teach a gospel that deviates from the one handed down to us from the apostles. About any teaching we can ask, "Is it consistent with what the prophets taught in the Old

Testament and what Jesus and the apostles taught in the New Testament?" While Paul, in his role as an apostle, could speak of "my" gospel, we can't.

2. "There are at least three dimensions to 'Paul's' gospel: (1) that salvation is in Jesus Christ alone, in fulfillment of the revelation given through Moses in millennia past; (2) that one becomes accepted by God solely by faith, apart from living in accordance with the law of Moses; and (3) that this acceptance and church participation is open as much to Gentiles as it is to Jews. While the first two have been the focus of theologians since the Reformation, the center of attention in Paul's day was the third. It was Gentile inclusion into justification by faith in Christ apart from the law that was the bone of contention between Paul and the Jerusalem Judaizers. Justification in Christ was acceptable to the Judaizers (after all, they claimed to be Christians). Justification for Gentiles was tolerable as well (Jews had plenty of precedent for conversion to Judaism by Gentiles). But it was justification before God *without obedience to the law of Moses* that became intolerable. This view threatened the very existence of Judaism and created the social crisis behind the letter."[1]

3. The introduction to this study guide addresses this question. Christ plus anything undermines the sufficiency of Christ and the Spirit. If God accepts us because of Christ's death plus something else, then Christ's death wasn't decisive.

4. The former age of practicing Judaism wasn't evil, but it's evil by comparison to the glorious age of Christ and the Spirit. Living as a BC person in an AD era is evil because it dismisses what Christ accomplished.

5. Questions 6 through 8 give some examples.

6. Such a person believes he is justified by faith but fails to understand what Paul means by "faith." As we'll see in future sessions, "faith" for Paul is more than just assent to some ideas. "I was once told by a well-meaning Sunday school teacher that it did not matter how I lived morally. If I was a Christian (defined as someone who had accepted Jesus Christ as Savior by performing a certain prayer), then I was eternally secure and could live any way I chose.... [This] is both inconsistent with the gospel and with the way the New Testament describes the effects of salvation. The gospel brings transformation (see 5:16–26). In other words, the original statement of the gospel may have been accurate: salvation is by grace through

faith, not by works. But the implications drawn from it were nonapostolic: live the way you want. The apostles never drew the conclusion that some Christians do today, namely, that lifestyle is totally disconnected from faith and salvation."[2]

7. When we emphasize the gospel's call for transformation, we need to make sure people don't lose "confidence in the sufficiency of Christ.... What we need, in all of this, is a balance that comes only as a result of God's grace, a balanced appreciation of both God's grace and the demand that grace has upon our lives. We must preach both God's grace and the transforming powers of the gospel."[3]

8. Christ's death on the cross for our sins is not only *sufficient* for our salvation, it's *essential*. In our pluralistic society today, many of us have family and friends of other faiths, and it's disturbing to think of them facing God's judgment. Like the Judaizers, we're tempted to tweak the gospel in order to avoid its disturbing aspects.

9. Paul invoked strong curses on those who distort the gospel (1:8–9). "The ancient world simply loved inflammatory language for expressing its differences."[4] That sort of thing comes across very differently today, so "What we need today is less tirade, less emotional outburst, and much more carefully constructed arguments that vindicate the truthfulness of the gospel of Jesus Christ."[5]

10. For example, rules can help young people learn what love, holiness, and self-control look like. They can help to form a conscience or help people become aware of their sinfulness. But it's important to avoid sending the message that (a) keeping the rules is what makes one acceptable to God, to the church, or to the family or (b) that keeping the rules is an effective substitute for learning to listen to and obey the Holy Spirit. Most parents have no idea how to train their children or teens to listen to the Holy Spirit for moral guidance. Rules should be part of that job, not a substitute for it.

11. It's essential to stay true to what the apostles have handed down to us as the truth, and to what we believe the Holy Spirit is guiding us to do. Often that involves listening to the wisdom of peers and elders. The Holy Spirit speaks to us not just as we pray alone, but also through the Scriptures and fellow Christians.

Sometimes, heeding the Holy Spirit means not making other people happy. But sometimes when we go against people in the belief that God is guiding us, we're wrong. "We can learn from such decisions, either to be more attentive to the Spirit of God or to listen to the wisdom of others; but nonetheless it is important that each Christian learn to live in the light of what God's will is."[6]

NOTES

1. McKnight, 63–64.
2. McKnight, 69.
3. McKnight, 53.
4. McKnight, 60.
5. Ibid.
6. McKnight, 68.

SESSION 2 LEADER'S NOTES

1. Peter (Cephas), James, and John declared Paul's message complete, they extended him the right hand of fellowship, they agreed that God had called Paul to take the gospel to the Gentiles, and they didn't require Titus to be circumcised. This last was important, because the Judaizers claimed that the Jerusalem leaders expected Gentile converts to be circumcised. The other apostles approved of what Paul said and didn't endorse the Judaizers.

2. To circumcise Titus would have been to tell him that he was obliged to keep the whole law of Moses. It would have said that he needed something other than the work of Christ and the guidance of the Holy Spirit to make him acceptable to God. For Paul, the law didn't free a Gentile from the clutches of paganism; it only subjected him to the curse the law pronounced upon sinners (3:10).

3. By ceasing to eat Gentile food with Gentiles, Peter was acting as if they needed to do something more than put their faith in Christ in order to be accepted by God and God's apostles. He was acting as if they needed to become Jewish (through circumcision) and live like Jews in order to be acceptable.

4. By treating the Gentiles as if they weren't acceptable, Peter was both yielding to and applying social pressure to make the Gentiles do whatever it took to become acceptable. He was humiliating and rejecting them, and because he carried the authority of an apostle, he was sending the message that God rejected them too. Anyone who has ever felt that kind of social pressure knows how forceful its effects can be.

5. Think of litmus tests you've seen Christians apply to assess whether other Christians are Christian enough. Also, think about the level of peer pressure in your group and your church. Are there unspoken expectations that pressure people to conform to your church's version of the faith? Is your group a safe place for group members to say they disagree with you or your church about Bible translations, the end times, politics? It would be good to find a way to talk about this in the group, to make sure your group isn't a place where peer pressure limits the work of the Holy Spirit.

6. Jews are justified by putting their faith in Christ. So are Gentiles, but Paul is speaking here particularly of Jews, as 2:15 shows.

7. This is no small task. People don't acquire an awareness of guilt by our lecturing them. We need to pray for God's grace to break through and convict them, both individually and society-wide. We need to teach the truth of God's ethical standards clearly, without apology, but also without hostility to those who don't get it. We need to dialogue with others about morality. Questions and genuine listening, undergirded by genuine relationship, can get through to some people over time. "Until our society awakens morally, it will be difficult to apply the doctrine of justification. But, as any evangelist will tell you, there are many today who are searching for answers to moral questions and to a consciousness of personal sin."[1]

8. If people believe the former, they may see doctrinal accuracy as important but holy living as optional and therefore not too important. This is one reason why statistics of sexual and financial sin among churchgoers and professing Christians are so close to statistics of the society as a whole.

   But if people understand that faith includes a continual response of trust, surrender, and obedience, they should be much more eager to ask questions like, "What does God want me to do? How can I become a person who lives the way God wants? How can the Holy Spirit help me?" Pursuing holiness then becomes a priority that takes time and other resources.

   Defining faith so that it includes surrender and obedience may make some in your group skeptical. It will be a good idea to watch how Paul speaks of faith in the rest of Galatians. We encourage you to read pages 119–123 in the commentary as well as other sections that address the definition of faith. We also encourage you to pay close attention to what Paul says in the rest of Galatians about *doing* things by faith.

9. By these definitions, to be justified by faith is to be set free from the penalty of sin because of our total trust and surrender to Jesus Christ, a trust and surrender that involves believing what the Scriptures teach, who he is, and what he has done, and that also involves doing what he says to do.

10. Again, you might want to consult the full argument in the commentary, and also stay tuned to study what Paul says in Galatians 5–6 about how Christians live.

11. Some of us have to die to knowing the minutia of right doctrine, because perfect knowledge is not necessary for God's acceptance. Likewise, being perfectly loving all the time is desirable, but God wants us to consistently

seek to grow in love by the power of his Spirit and to honestly admit our failures. And being perfect in the sense of never doing anything embarrassing is completely irrelevant to God, so if we're perfectionists, we need to die to that too.

NOTE

1. McKnight, 128.

SESSION 3 LEADER'S NOTES

1. The crucial question is repeated: The Galatians have experienced the Holy Spirit at and since their conversion, long before they started dabbling in the law.

2. Paul can exhort people who already have the Spirit (Eph. 4:30) to seek to be filled with the Spirit (Eph. 5:18), but we see no evidence in Paul that receiving Christ and receiving the Spirit for the first time can be separate events. If we're correct about that, then it should be normal for every Christian to live in the power of the Spirit. That many professing Christians don't appear to be doing so suggests that the gospel they've been taught may be deficient. They need to learn how the Spirit operates and how they can cooperate.

3. "By 'charismatic' I simply mean that the Galatians may have spoken in tongues, displayed miracles, or been given prophetic utterances as demonstrations of the presence of the Holy Spirit. Historians of the early churches are well aware of the amount of charismatic activity that took place, for which we find evidence in Acts (cf. Acts 2–3; 8; 10; 18) and in the debates arising at Corinth (cf. 1 Cor. 12–14). Charismatic phenomena were neither unique nor surprising in the early churches."[1] Christians differ as to which, if any, of these phenomena we should expect to experience today. But we agree that the Spirit still brings conviction of sin and the desire to live a holy life. Where those are absent, the authenticity of even the most memorable experience is open to doubt.

4. Living by the Spirit involves more effort than just going on autopilot in our well-worn habits. There's the effort of setting aside distractions and making time to listen to the Spirit through reading and reflecting on the Scripture, and through prayer. There's the effort of paying attention to our lives—both what happens to us and how we respond—to discern what the Spirit may be saying to us. There's the effort of inviting feedback from other believers and listening to what they have to say. These and many other "disciplines" don't make us more acceptable to God but can help us hear and follow the Spirit.

5. They need to know that these ideas are not novelties Paul dreamed up that are inconsistent with Scripture.

6. Abraham's faith consistently involved action, often costly action. We wouldn't say he had faith in God if he had stayed in Ur and simply believed true doctrines about God.

7. Paul teaches three truths about the gospel: "(1) people are by nature slaves to sin and under the curse of the law, (2) Christ paid the price of freedom by dying on the cross, and (3) those who trust in Christ's ransom price are set free from sin and the curse of the law.

    "How did Christ do this? Christ ransomed Jewish Christians from the curse of the law 'by becoming a curse.' What Christ did was to die the death of a transgressor (this is the point of quoting Deut. 21:23). In so doing, he becomes the transgressor because Christ was publicly crucified (cf. 2 Cor. 5:21). But because he was innocent and sinless, he can die on behalf of those who have sinned and so absorb their curse. And because he was divine, he could perfectly satisfy the justice of God (see Rom. 3:21–26)."[2]

8. He became a curse by dying the death of a transgressor and taking the transgressions on himself.

9. "[W]e do not operate with a Christian reading of Scripture if we do not see God's promises in Abraham as critical and fulfilled in Christ. Christ's work is not something totally new; it is the climactic fulfillment of the promises given to Abraham....

    "[M]ost of us read the Bible in a highly *individual manner*. We read the Bible for personal blessing, personal guidance, and personal instruction, and we should. But sometimes our individual desires express a rank egocentric approach to life and Bible reading....

    "Second, we often read the Bible *apart from contexts*. Perhaps this is a result of the convention of a Bible separated into verses rather than paragraphs. Many Christians today like to read the Bible as if it were all like Proverbs—that is, as if it contained nothing but random sayings that have almost no connection to one another."[3]

10. For example, many people today are completely unaware that they practice idolatry, that they treat things as ultimate that are not in fact ultimate. Perhaps they worship youth, beauty, wealth, and fame. They may even worship those qualities embodied in a celebrity. They don't even know they do this, let alone that there's anything wrong with it. But the command, "I

am the LORD your God … You shall have no other gods before me" (Ex. 20:2–3) reveals that this behavior is wrong in the eyes of the God who gave the law. Exodus even depicts vividly why the behavior is wrong.

11. He wants them to value it for what it can still offer in the age of Christ, neither dismissing it nor subjecting themselves to it.

12. Some of the laws here, such as Leviticus 19:1 or 19:18, express foundational principles that are repeated in the New Testament. Laws against disrespect for parents, idolatry, theft, lying, deception, fraud, exploitation of workers, disrespect for the disabled, and so on sketch a picture of what God sees as right and wrong. It's worthwhile to investigate why mixing different fibers in the same cloth (19:19) and tattooing the body (19:28) were forbidden, but that doesn't mean taking such prohibitions wholesale into our Christian lives.

13. "[F]ew Christians today believe that the Spirit of God is the central focus for Christian ethics. I believe, in fact, that Christians treat the New Testament more like a second Mosaic law than as a witness to God's Spirit leading his new people. Paul saw the Judaizers as 'law-centered,' and he wanted a church of people who were 'Spirit-centered.' But we cannot be detained by this perspective, since we are assuming that Christians do believe in the Spirit's guidance, can follow it, and will do what God's Spirit says."[4] Christians who don't know how to listen to the Spirit's guidance or can't be trusted to follow it desperately need to be trained.

Responding to God's Word: McKnight talks about the value of looking at our experience, but also about how experiences can be deceiving (143–144). We need to assess them in light of Scripture. Some group members may have trouble articulating any experience of the Spirit. That may be because they aren't Christians—they are in mental agreement to some ideas but haven't ever really surrendered themselves to God. But equally it could be that they associate the Spirit with impressive displays. When have they seen fruit in their lives? When have they seen God guiding them, convicting them? When have they found themselves able to surrender the whole of themselves to what God was doing and sign on to serve him despite the cost?

NOTES

1. McKnight, 138–139.
2. McKnight, 156–157.
3. McKnight, 171–172.
4. McKnight, 188–189.

SESSION 4 LEADER'S NOTES

1. "[I]n Christ there are no racial, social, or sexual distinctions, because all are one."[1] All who have been baptized into Christ are God's adult children/sons and heirs. This offer is available to all, but only those who accept it by surrendering their lives to Christ will inherit it.

   About Paul's statement in 3:28 that in Christ there is neither slave nor free, male nor female, see McKnight, 200–202, 205–214. This study doesn't address the implications of Paul's words for modern relationships between men and women, because that subject would need a session on its own to bridge from ancient to modern culture, and because this is not Paul's main emphasis in Galatians. But such a discussion is well worth having.

2. We develop intimacy with God through prayer — prayer that explores God's relationship to us and our relationship to God, prayer that is trusting and vulnerable to God's promise and sure word, and prayer that is designed to live before God obediently and lovingly. We develop intimacy with God through a lifestyle that remains in consistent conversation with God as each day progresses. Instead of diddling away our time with thoughts of fleeting things as we drive the car or wash the dishes or go for walks, we can spend our time in those activities talking to God and listening to him speak to us as his children. We can pray and learn to know God.

   We also develop intimacy with God by reading his Word, believing it, obeying it, and sharing it with others. But mostly, we learn to be intimate with God by trusting in him and learning through that trust that he is loving and good.[2]

3. Foremost in Paul's mind is that we care far less about our social status compared to that of other people — about how much money we make or what the car we drive says about us, about whether our children's achievements impress others. And we stop measuring others by how well they speak English, what they wear, or how much money they have. We're grateful for being in Christ, and that gratitude overcomes our insecurities. Many actions that flow from this could be listed. For example, we could probably spend less money on ourselves and give more away to the work of God.

4. "The development today of the 'black gospel' and the 'Hispanic gospel' is, in my view, a distortion caused by what is taken to be *the* gospel: the

'white gospel.' When whites learn that the gospel they believe has been shaped massively by their white culture, we shall make progress."[3] This "white gospel" is shaped by cultural pressure for whites to live by the social customs of white suburbia, much as Jews in Paul's day were expected to live like Jews. "What Paul teaches is that the gospel of Jesus Christ is for all, all together, not all apart or each in its racial quarter. The issue separating Paul's gospel from the Judaizer's gospel was as much Jewish versus Gentile as it was Moses versus Jesus. And the issue separating black and white today is as much racial as it is religious. In fact, I would say that it is ninety percent racial; the religious elements separating blacks and whites are hardly known (besides whites being stiff in their worship style)."[4]

5. We see the close connections among the persons of the Trinity here: The Spirit is called "the Spirit of his Son." The Father sends the Spirit. The Spirit calls out "Abba." All of this happens because we have faith in the Son. All three persons are involved, inseparable yet distinct. To have the Son without the Spirit is unimaginable for Paul. Ditto the Father without the Spirit, or foregrounding the Spirit while downplaying Father and Son.

6. Nearly every sentence expresses frustration, anguish, exasperation. "How is it that ... weak and miserable ...? You are observing ...!"

7. Some people are more naturally passionate than others, and that's fine. This is a chance for group members to assess whether they are too zealous, or not zealous enough, or zealous about the wrong things.

8. Paul wanted the Galatian converts to grow in the Spirit until the image of Christ was formed—actually "transformed"—in them (cf. Rom. 12:1–2; 13:14; Eph. 4:23–24; Col. 1:24–2:5; 3:10).[5]

9. "Paul's goal was not to have people say he was a great evangelist; not to have the approval of others; not to have the sanction of Jerusalem. His goal in working with people was to have Christ formed in them."[6]

10. Identifying the Jews as the sons of the slave woman, as not being children of promise. Associating Mount Sinai and earthly Jerusalem with slavery. It's no wonder Paul's kinsmen came to hate him as a traitor.

11. The childish state of being under the law is slavery. Being under pagan gods is equally slavery. Freedom is being adopted as one of God's adult children. Faith is freeing. Having the Spirit is freedom. Being able to call God "Abba" is freedom.

12. Use this question to explore how members of the group see room for improvement in their relationship with God in light of Paul's message.

NOTES

1. McKnight, 196.
2. McKnight, 212.
3. McKnight, 163.
4. Ibid.
5. McKnight, 221.
6. McKnight, 224.

SESSION 5 LEADER'S NOTES

1. For a fuller treatment of this view of freedom, see McKnight, 242–247, 253–261. It will be worthwhile to spend time exploring what group members really believe about freedom, because freedom is one of the top values in our culture, and the gap between our culture's definition and Paul's is wide. Our understanding of freedom greatly affects the goals we pursue, the personal choices we make, even the way we vote.

2. "[F]reedom surely involves the tearing down of social injustices. There are many politicians whose sole goal in life is this kind of freedom, and we should applaud their efforts on our behalf. Such obstacles naturally include environmental issues that foster tension in communities, racial prejudices that determine public policies, sexual discrimination that influences pay scales, and international imperialism that can keep some countries from development or force weaker nations down on the economic ladder. Such injustices need to be opposed, and the work for freedom in these areas is altogether good.

    "But there often comes an imbalance.... While social freedom is certainly an aspect of the Pauline notion of freedom, it is not the totality, and for liberation theologians and activists the concept of freedom is far too materialistic to embrace the fullness of the biblical variety of evidence."[1]

    "Social justice is not an end in itself; it is a means of declaring the work of God for the Christian."[2]

3. This question assesses how well the group has taken in Paul's argument in previous sessions. Law-keeping is fine as a cultural expression of Jewishness, but not if one views it as essential to God's acceptance. To deny Christ's sufficiency is to reject his grace. Law-keeping is also a problem if it keeps Jewish and Gentile Christians from eating and worshiping together, because that denies our oneness in Christ.

4. Salvation has both an "already" and a "not yet" dimension. We are already justified/made righteous in that Christ has already paid the penalty for our sin and God has already erased the "felony charges" against us. But we are not yet fully justified/made righteous in that when God is finished transforming us and we are ready for resurrection, our inclination to sin will be gone as well.

5. Paul gives us cause to wonder whether that kind of faith is real saving faith: "'those who live like this [as described in 5:19–21] will not inherit the kingdom of God' (v. 21). Whether a person made some kind of profession of faith, whether a person had a charismatic experience, or whether a person endured a great deal of suffering does not matter *if he or she lives in the flesh* (cf. Matt. 7:15–27; 2 Cor. 5:10; James 2:14–26). One's final standing before God, Paul contends, is directly related to whether or not a person lives in the flesh or in the Spirit."[3]

6. Habits of self-indulgence take on lives of their own, and we lose the capacity to say no to them. The language of addiction has spread from dependencies on chemical substances like alcohol or heroin to encompass habits like sexual promiscuity, use of pornography, compulsive shopping, and uncontrolled anger. Any habit we can't simply decide to stop is one that has enslaved us. If limiting shopping (for example) makes us sad, anxious, or angry, then it is likely an area of slavery.

7. For example, walking in the Spirit involves deciding upfront in a given situation that one will do whatever the Spirit wants, even if that goes against one's vested interests or looking good in front of other people. It means surrendering one's agenda to the Spirit. It means being willing to change one's mind, even in front of other people. We often know what the Bible says about our desires; the struggle is choosing to act accordingly.

   Walking in the Spirit also means taking time to listen to the Spirit through pondering what the Bible says. Chewing on a story or a statement. Thinking about it throughout the day. Praying over it. Making space in one's life for silence and solitude, not because those acts will make God accept us more, but because they help us hear him. Making time to talk with other believers about what's going on in our lives and what God might be up to, and listening to their questions and reflections.

   "I believe that the Spirit of the Lord guides us usually in one of four ways: through circumstances, through other Christians, through the Bible, and through prayer and/or spiritual intuition.... The issue, however, remains the same: Do we really believe God's Spirit is a sufficient guide?"[4]

8. "[I]t is not that Paul did not have available rules and regulations to appeal to: he could have gone to Moses for some moral guidelines or even to Jesus.

He could have appealed to such texts as the Sermon on the Mount (Matt. 5–7) or to specific texts in the Old Testament (e.g., Lev. 11:44–45: 'Be holy, because I am holy'). He did not, however, and he knew that in not doing so he was leaving these as options [i.e., alternative choices to the gospel]. He did not see the teachings of Jesus as new laws, nor would he appeal to the law of Moses as binding on the Christian. Instead, Paul described the essence of Christian living as 'freedom in the Spirit.'

"To be sure, Paul knew that when a person was controlled by the Spirit, that person was holy.... Thus, he knew that the Old Testament moral guidelines and the teachings of Jesus on holiness, righteousness, and compassion would be confirmed by anyone who lived in the Spirit.... However, even with this important qualification, Paul stressed that true living before God was a life in the Spirit and a life of spiritual freedom. The question for us is direct: Is our ethic an ethic of freedom in the Spirit or is it much more like that of the Judaizing invaders?"[5]

9–10. The fact that many Christians have no idea how transformation in the Holy Spirit takes place helps to explain why we see less transformation than we should. Everything said above under question 7 applies here. If we're listening to the Holy Spirit through the Scriptures, other people, etc., and if we're open to letting him convict us, he will show us sinful patterns in the way we relate to others. He will also guide and empower us through a process of acquiring different habits of mind and behavior. One of the church's main jobs is to teach members how transformation happens and to support them in surrendering to the Spirit.

One important habit we need to acquire is noticing and labeling fleshly desires when they occur to us. That desire to deceive someone or to see them get what's coming to them — simply recognizing such desires of the sinful nature and handing them over to the Spirit is a small but important first step.

11. Many churches do an inadequate job of teaching members how transformation in the Spirit happens. Churches may fail to train Christians in the habits of cooperating with the Spirit and to support them as they seek to do so. They may fail to explain that unwillingness to be transformed isn't a real option for a Christian, and fail to recognize and to treat behaviors like jealousy and discord as sins that are as serious as sexual immorality.

Too many churches teach members that simply believing the right information about Jesus is sufficient, so members don't even know they need to surrender the habits of their sinful nature to the Spirit.

NOTES

1. McKnight, 255–256.
2. McKnight, 260.
3. McKnight, 270, italics original.
4. McKnight, 280.
5. McKnight, 273.

SESSION 6 LEADER'S NOTES

1. Restore sinners gently—that is, humbly. Guard yourself against sinful pride, which is self-deception. Carry the sinner's burden—that is, help the sinner break free from the sin. Evaluate yourself not by comparing yourself to the sinner—which is all too easy to do—but to what the Spirit is asking of you. Take responsibility for your own sins and help others with theirs.

2. "Gentleness" is humility. A humble person avoids humiliating the sinner and so helps the sinner face his misdeed honestly. Harsh or belittling words, such as "I told you so," hinder rather than help repentance. It's sometimes necessary to remove people from positions of authority or privilege when they do something seriously wrong, but we needn't dismantle their dignity in the process.

3. Paul says the arrogant are nothing and deceive themselves. They should pay attention to their own actions and be aware that they too will be judged by their deeds.

4. "Mutual accountability forces many of us to abandon our sense of being alone and forces us to reach out to others. It makes the neighbor stand up and say, 'I truly am a neighbor and must be neighborly.' It makes the person abandon the natural (modern) impulse of letting all others do their own thing.... It also forces the neighbor to allow his or her life to be open enough to others ... to be a neighbor in a genuine sense....

   "Our personal responsibility before God does not relieve us from accountability to others, nor does it put us on a deserted island to live a solitary life. These are Western problems that need to be faced."[1]

5. Test your own actions. Carry your own load. You'll reap what you sow. Don't get weary of doing good.

6. We are justified by faith in Christ. The issue here is, what does it mean to have faith in Christ? Does it mean only to mentally assent to a set of ideas about him? Or does it include living a life of surrender to him?

   " 'How can a loving God punish?' [some] ask. The answer ... is context. The God of love in the Bible is also a God who is altogether holy and who will never act contrary to his holy and loving nature. Thus, the only foundation for acceptance with God is his method: his Son, Jesus Christ, expressed God's love in dying for us, but he had to die for us because God is holy (Rom. 3:21–25 discusses this). This means that God's justice is expressed in the cross as much as God's love is."[2]

This shouldn't terrify us, but should motivate us to learn how to walk by the Spirit. "Paul says that God will judge us *on the basis of our life*, whether it was 'in the Spirit' or 'in the flesh.' ... To be sure ... the basis of our acceptance with God is what Christ has done on our behalf. But for God to assess whether we are attached to Christ, he will simply scan the evidence of our lives: Is it one of living 'in the Spirit' or of living 'in the flesh'? Those who live 'in the Spirit' do so by faith and obedience; those who live 'in the flesh' have sins aplenty to show for their time on earth. "The judgment of God, then, is a motivational force for the Christian."[3]

7. "In our culture we have become acutely aware of the origins and causes of our behavior.... But in this process, at times *there is an implicit excuse* for our personality traits or our behavior.... 'You would not blame me if you knew my past.' We must sympathize here with the obvious reality that what we do and who we are result from what others have made us, and we should not refrain from recognizing that certain bad dimensions of people are not solely their fault. But what the Bible teaches is that *we are personally responsible for everything we are and for everything we do, regardless of the causes and problems we might have*. This, of course, leads to an entire feature of application: urging people to accept responsibility for everything they do and are. Paul teaches that we must 'bear our own burdens' in this regard."[4] Genes or childhood trauma may partially explain a sinful pattern of behavior, and we should have compassion on one another for these reasons. But these aren't excuses; we are each responsible to cooperate with the Spirit in the sometimes extremely painful and difficult process of becoming free from a sinful pattern.

8. One example: "I have seen this kind of pressure exerted even today with the rite of adult immersion, where pastors and leaders and 'significant others' have put considerable pressure on people to get them to admit their infant baptism was inadequate. At times, I have seen such people surrender to this force solely to avoid social shame — disrespecting their own conscience in the matter."[5] Baptism is important — in the early church it was *"the initial and necessary response of faith,"*[6] a dramatization of salvation (see 3:27). Unbaptized believers were unknown. Still, telling

people they aren't fully Christians if they haven't been baptized the "right way" is an error.

9. Too often in a church it only takes one or two strong personalities to get the more passive people to go along, and often the strong can scare the passive people into putting pressure on others.

10. If we boast not in our achievements but in Christ's, we risk getting less approval from other people than we would if we made their approval a priority. We may get less attention, have less status, even make less money. We need to be honest about these potential costs, or we'll balk at living in the Spirit when the costs start mounting.

NOTES

1. McKnight, 290–291.
2. McKnight, 296.
3. Ibid., italics original.
4. McKnight, 291, italics original.
5. McKnight, 300.
6. McKnight, 198, italics original.

The NIV Application Commentary

Galatians

Scot McKnight

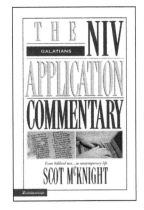

Most Bible commentaries take us on a one-way trip from our world to the world of the Bible. But they leave us there, assuming that we can somehow make the return journey on our own. In other words, they focus on the original meaning of the passage but don't discuss its contemporary application. The information they offer is valuable — but the job is only half done!

The NIV Application Commentary series helps us with both halves of the interpretative task. This new and unique series shows readers how to bring an ancient message into a modern context. It explains not only what the Bible meant but also how it can speak powerfully today.

It was the apostle Paul's approach to visionary leadership that enabled him to confront the burning question of Galatians: the relationship of the Mosaic law to the gospel of Jesus Christ. As Scot McKnight so expertly details, Paul challenged the Galatians' mistaken understanding of the law. They were, in effect, creating a new gospel. Had Paul been content to focus on leadership technique and style and to list his leadership accomplishments in the standard way, he would have been implicitly using the same methodology as the Judaizers. Instead, at every possible point, Paul pointed away from himself toward Jesus Christ.

Hardcover, Printed: 978-0-310-48470-7

Pick up a copy at your favorite bookstore or online!

Share Your Thoughts

With the Author: Your comments will be forwarded to the author when you send them to *zauthor@zondervan.com*.

With Zondervan: Submit your review of this book by writing to *zreview@zondervan.com*.

Free Online Resources at
www.zondervan.com

Zondervan AuthorTracker: Be notified whenever your favorite authors publish new books, go on tour, or post an update about what's happening in their lives at www.zondervan.com/authortracker.

Daily Bible Verses and Devotions: Enrich your life with daily Bible verses or devotions that help you start every morning focused on God. Visit www.zondervan.com/newsletters.

Free Email Publications: Sign up for newsletters on Christian living, academic resources, church ministry, fiction, children's resources, and more. Visit www.zondervan.com/newsletters.

Zondervan Bible Search: Find and compare Bible passages in a variety of translations at www.zondervanbiblesearch.com.

Other Benefits: Register yourself to receive online benefits like coupons and special offers, or to participate in research.

■ ZONDERVAN®

ZONDERVAN.com/
AUTHORTRACKER
follow your favorite authors

Printed in the USA
CPSIA information can be obtained
at www.ICGtesting.com
LVHW021356241223
767279LV00010B/111